Kids Guide

to

Movie Making

How kids can produce & direct their
own movies that audiences will love

Published by Make-A-Movie Studios
www.makeamoviestudios.com
For ordering information:
650-906-8296
shelley@makeamoviestudios.com

Printed and bound by Createspace

ISBN:1456525069
ISBN-13:978-1456525064

Kids Guide

to

Movie Making

How kids can produce & direct their own
movies that audiences will love

by Shelley Frost

DEDICATION

With undying thanks to my mom
Nancy Ruff who patiently
attended and warmly applauded
my many plays, puppet shows
and movies.

Contents

Chapter One   8
    Why Make A Movie?
        Special Welcome by Shelley Frost

Chapter Two   11
    The FOUR Stages of Movie Making
        Pre-Production
        Production
        Post-Production
        Premier Your Movie

Chapter Three   17
    Your Role as a Movie Director

Chapter Four   22
    Make Your Movie Plan (Pre-Production)
        Script, Storyboards, Production
        Schedule

Chapter Five   31
    Make Your Movie (Production)
    Equipment, Movie Set Jobs, Locations,
    Directing Actors, Directing Your Movie,
    Shooting Tips, Types of Shots, Bloopers,
    Special Effects while Shooting

Chapter Six   54
    Edit Your Movie (Post-Production)

Chapter Seven   57
    Premier Your Movie

Shelley's Greenlight   59

Sample Movie Making Materials   60

Chapter One
Why Make-A-Movie?

Kids! Your imaginations are like overflowing ice cream sundae's with rivers of chocolate and carmel syrup, towering peaks of whipped cream, trails of chopped nuts and juicy sweet cherries. The ideas, stories and pictures in your mind are bubbling and swirling, just like a generous ice cream dessert.

Just as you would never let that sundae melt away to nothing, you should never let the stories in your imagination, melt away to nothing. So what do you do with these stories?

Make a movie!

Making a movie means telling a story. Remember what it's like having a story book read out loud to you? What is happening in your mind while the person's words flow through your imagination? It's like you're watching your very own, private movie!

HOT TIP!

Throughout this book, you will see highlighted sections titled HOT TIP! These are special insights learned by movie directors while on set, that are now being passed along to you. These bits of movie making wisdom should help you have a more successful movie making experience.

My name is Shelley Frost and I've been a Movie Director for kids since 2002.   I've produced and directed over 100 movies starring over 1,000 kids. Everything I've learned about movie making and working with casts and crews of kids your age is right here in this book.

I have directed the kids of Hollywood parents such as Michelle Pfeiffer and Leah Remini. I have been a drama teacher for several nieces and a nephew of Gore Verbinski, the director of *Pirates of the Caribbean* movies. Another student of mine now has a career in Broadway plays in New York City.

So if you believe you have what it takes to produce and direct a movie from start to finish, this book will help you make it happen. If you make it to the end, you will get my green light!

Chapter Two

The FOUR Stages of Movie Making

Most books and movie making articles you read will tell you there are three stages of movie making: Pre-production, production and post-production. But we've added a fourth, probably the most important stage, and that is **premiering your movie**.

Because when your movie is screened (or shown) is when the all important audience is in the picture. And as you read this book, you will constantly be reminded to never forget the most important people attached to your movie, and that is your audience!

1. Pre-Production - this is the easiest and most stress free part of making a movie. You are doing it right now just by reading this book!

During pre-production you will choose your script, make your cast and crew lists, think about your locations and hopefully gather a few dollars for your movie budget.

You will also begin reaching out to your friends and family asking them to participate as an actor, crew member or donor of supplies. If you plan to have auditions, you will plan and hold these events too.

You will also think about where you will find your props and costumes. Use your e-mail lists or Facebook account to start searching for the items you need. Hopefully people will gladly donate these things which will keep your budget very low. Make sure they put their names on all donated items that they wish returned to them.

2. *Production:* This is the time when all the pieces of your movie project happen in real time. It is also the time when you will face many challenges that will make or break the completion of your movie. With a smile on your face and determination in your heart, don't let any of the following stumbling blocks trip you up.

PEOPLE: Did you choose the right people for the right roles? The people you surround yourself with will be the biggest unpredictable element throughout your movie project - more so even than the weather (more on that next!).

If you doubt someone's ability, dedication or temperament, it may be in your movie's best interest to not have them on board. Be tough but fair in your decisions regarding who will be on your cast and crew.

WEATHER: Can you deal with a day of bad weather, shooting interior scenes instead of exterior scenes?

MONEY: And then the dicey subject of money. Can you film and edit your entire movie with the money you have (not the money you wished you had)?

3. Post-Production: Holding your precious cassettes of shot film, you enter the darkened interior of the edit room. Do you have a good editor who is knowledgeable in using Final Cut Pro or another stable video editing software platform?

Beyond the initial edit of pairing down your many hours of shot footage into a 90 minute or less film, you will need to think about the sound. Are the footsteps down the stone stairway loud enough? Can you hear your lead actress's voice over the sound of a nearby running car engine?

HOT TIP!

While on set, always have a notepad that you can jot down important notes such as the following: "While Miranda was saying opening lines, airplane flying overhead. Check if need voice over."

In post-production, this is also the time you add music. Ideally, you can create original music tracks either by recording original music or by creating tracks on a software program such as Apple's Garageband.

If you plan to distribute your movie beyond your own neighborhood OR you plan to upload it onto a website or YouTube, you need to have the rights to any music you use in your movie.

The easiest way around this is to create brand new, original music that only you have the rights to.

Listed at the back of this book are websites that license music to film makers. Their licensing fees can be anywhere from $20 per track up to hundreds of dollars per track.

4. Premier your movie: Premiering your movie before a live audience can be the most thrilling moment and the most frightening. Your heart will leap with joy when they laugh at the exact right moment. And when the lights come back on and you find yourself surrounded by well wishers full of praise and compliments, there is no better feeling in the world.

To experience this, you must arrange to show your movie preferably where there is a large screen and good sound system.

This could be your own house or a friends house or the local movie theater! If you are interested in raising money for your favorite charity, you might consider selling tickets. Then again, you could also attempt to sell tickets and pocket the cash to cover your production expenses.

Hot Tip!

Call your local library to see if they have a "media room" available for public use that you can reserve to show your movie. Librarians often will help you promote the movie premier.

If you can, offer popcorn and drinks. Allow time for a question answer session with you and your cast. No matter what, it will be a night you will never forget.

Hot Tip!

Check out film festivals where you can submit your film to be considered for competitions. Without A Box (www.withoutabox.com) is a clearing house of all international and national film festivals and provides all the contact information you need to submit your movie.

Chapter Three

Your Role as *The* Movie Director

As a movie director, you use a camera to film the stories living in your imagination. Next, you show your movie to an audience. If you hear their applause, you will know you've succeeded as a movie director. (Let's not even think about an unhappy audience!).

What is a movie director? This is the person in charge of bringing a movie to life - from the pages of the script to the screen at the movie theater. The director uses his or her actors, along with the props, costumes and locations to tell a complete story.

The director is responsible for everything that makes a movie successful. If you are the movie director, then you are the boss.

A great movie is:
A movie audiences will want to watch.

17

A movie they will recommend to their friends and family.

A movie that critics will adore.

A movie that will win you an award or two!

A great movie director is:

Someone with a clear vision of how their movie should look, sound and feel.

Someone who enjoys working with people.

Someone who appreciates the talents of others.

Someone who stays organized and can multi-task never giving up.

AND someone who knows how to talk!

You will be talking more than any other task you have as a movie director.

To be a great movie director you will

need to be a great communicator. This means knowing how to explain your vision to your cast and crew. Listen to their ideas. Give them positive feedback. And when problems or disagreements arise, it is your job to step in and solve them as fairly and quickly as possible.

Movies are filled with people both in front of the camera and behind the scenes. The better your people skills, the better chance your movie will come alive. This means respecting everyone contributing to the movie. Whether they are the lead actress or the script girl, listen to their ideas so they feel valued. This will ensure that your instruction to them will be welcomed, not ignored.

Hot Tip!

Movie Directors must rely on the talents of their cast and crew to bring their vision to life. Your number one talent will be how you use your voice when talking to the people on your movie set. For the best results, be supportive, compassionate and complimentary.

After the shooting is over, the movie director will shout, "Cut, that's a wrap!" Then the next stage of movie making begins: editing. Whether you work with an editor or do the editing yourself, this is a time consuming, technical process.

Today's computers and software make movie editing easier than ever. Using Apple's iMovie, Final Cut Pro or another program, you will organize all your shot footage into a sequence, add music, effects and titles. This is where you watch the vision of your movie flow from your imagination to the reality of the computer screen.

Now, are you ready to be a movie director? Find out by asking yourself these questions:

Do I understand the story I wish to tell to MY AUDIENCE?

Do I know what an audience will enjoy watching?

Am I a leader people will respond to?

Do I have the time and patience to shoot a movie?

Can I choose the right people to play the right characters?

Can I learn from my mistakes to make the next day's shoot better?

Am I ready to tackle the technical challenges of movie making?

Hot Tip!

Imagine you are sitting in a movie theater waiting for the lights to dim and the movie to start - your movie. But you are not you. You are a member of the audience who is only interested in sitting back, and being entertained. Will your movie give your audience an emotional experience? Will your movie keep an audience spellbound? Wanting more when the lights come back on? As you plan and produce your movie, never forget about your audience and their expectations.

Chapter Four

Make Your Movie Plan
(Pre-Production)

Another key role of the movie director is handling all the pre-production homework. These are the preparations you must make before the first day of shooting.

Start with a Great Movie Script
Anyone with a video camera and a few friends who like to mug faces and tell jokes can record something to videotape. But who is going to want to watch that so-called movie?

As a filmmaker, you are a storyteller. Your goal is to entertain and enlighten your audience. The best way to start making an entertaining and enlightening movie is by using a script with exciting characters, an intriguing plot, fascinating locations and meaningful props.

If you would like to write your own movie script, use our book KIDS GUIDE TO WRITING A MOVIE SCRIPT (Due to be published in 2011).

Another idea is to use a movie script from Make-A-Movie Studios (www.makeamoviestudios.com). There are many to choose from in a variety of genres.

A genre is a category or type of movie such as these: DRAMA, SCIENCE FICTION, ACTION, COMEDY, FANTASY, MYSTERY, ROMANCE.

Here is a sample of a few Make-A-Movie Studios scripts *(See the back of this book for sample pages from our movie scripts)*:

"A Spy in Mozambula" ACTION
"The Mystery of the Missing Soccer Trophy" MYSTERY
"The Princess & the Pickle Pie" FANTASY
"The Stroke of Midnight" HORROR/ SCARY

Once you've chosen your movie script, you will want to plow through it word by word, line by line. This is when you might make changes to dialogue, plan camera angles or list the props you will need.

Storyboards

Storyboards are a great tool that can help to keep you better organized and to make sure nothing is missed during your movie shoot.

Storyboards are drawings or rough sketches of the movie's scenes. These scetches will make to help you understand the flow of your movie. Once completed they look like a comic strip.

You can even include bubbles over character's heads filled with the words they are speaking.

Don't worry about your drawing abilities. Storyboards can be filled with stick figures and shapes. The purpose of storyboards is to give you an idea of how the shot will look. This could actually make the shooting day more efficient and successful.

A great movie director uses his or her storyboards almost like a coach uses his or her play book. But instead of football or basketball plays, you are constructing shot by shot layouts of how your movie will look and how you picture each shot.

But just as a coach fills a play book with notes and ideas, feel free to jot notes below your drawings, just as if they were captions beneath a picture. This way, your storyboards will help remind you of the wonderful ideas you had weeks before shooting started.

Your storyboards might be very elaborate, filled with depictions of special effects you've dreamed up. Or you can keep them simple, just showing the sequence of scenes that you plan to include. *(See the back of this book for sample storyboard layouts).*

Hot Tip!

While storyboarding, visualize your shots: Best composition - positioning of people and objects.
Best Lighting - dramatic, high or low? Best point of view - where the camera is positioned and what it is "seeing."

Once you are shooting your movie, you will refer to your storyboards just as you do the movie script. You might refer to a storyboard to remind you of a camera angle or a character's positioning or a key prop you had pencilled into a scene.

Excite your audience with fantastic opening credits!

Opening credits are the first impression your audience has of the movie they are about to watch. This is when you will launch them on the emotional roller coaster that is the story of your movie.

In planning your opening credit footage and music, think about the theme, messages or genre of your movie script.

For the Make-A-Movie Studios script "Where Are You Barkus Canis?" the story follows two young scientists determined to prove the existence of a small elusive forest creature named Barkus Canis. If they can prove the Barkus Canis is alive, the forest will be saved from evil real estate developers.

While shooting the opening credits, we placed our "Barkus Canis" (a stuffed life-like looking tiger) on tree branches, under bushes, behind rocks, and filmed just parts of the the animal. Combined with mysterious music and a few special effects, the opening credits gave the impression of a mystery that would take place in a dark, spooky forest.

Entertaining closing credits

Closing credits can be as simple as scrolling text listing the cast and crew's names. Or they can be exciting and fun, allowing the audience one last glimpse of the characters they grew to love while watching the movie.

A fun closing credits idea is to allow each actor to perform a 10 second action that mirrors something special about their character.

In the Make-A-Movie Studios script, "Where Are You Barkus Canis," the character Bridget, always uses a magnifying glass as she tramps through the forest looking for the Barkus Canis.

In her closing credit, we filmed an extreme close-up of the actor playing Bridget holding the magnifying glass close to her eyes, then pulling the camera back, so her whole smiling face came into view. Her name and character's name appeared just below her chin.

Plan Your Production Schedule
(See the back of this book for a sample production schedule)

Your production schedule should list the following:
> *Dates*
> *Times*
> *Locations*
> *Scenes to be shot (don't forget to include your opening & closing credits)*
> *Cast members on set*
> *Props & Costumes needed*

Ask yourself when do you plan to shoot your movie? Do you have a week off from school in the spring? Are there several weeks during the summer that you plan to film your movie?

Get out an oversized calendar, and begin planning your shooting days. The beauty of movie making is that you can jumble up the shooting of scenes and organize them later in the edit room.

28

In other words, movies are rarely shot in sequential order. Movies are shot when it is most convenient. If the sunset is exactly how you envisioned it to look in scene eight of your movie and you have just completed scene two, go ahead and shoot scene eight, capturing that incredible lighting.

Looking at your script, which scenes can you shoot together? Does scene one and scene ten take place at the same location? If so, then plan to shoot both scenes on that day. Or, if your lead actor is free only on Wednesday's plan all his scenes accordingly.

Create a spreadsheet on your computer with the entire production schedule laid out, then send a copy to everyone in your cast and crew (collect their contact information at your Cast Meeting - see below).

The FIRST DATE you will list on your production schedule is the Cast & Crew Introduction Meeting. Here is a sample agenda for your Cast & Crew Intro Meeting:
　　1. Introductions
　　　　Go around the room so everyone

can introduce themselves and say what part/
job they have in the movie.

    2. Send around the table (or room) a
clip board for everyone to write down their
contact info - phone number, e-mail
address.

    3. Quick lesson in how to make a
movie:

"Quiet on the Set" - when "Action!" is
called, everyone must be quiet; When
saying lines ALWAYS look at the person to
whom your character is speaking; never
look in the camera lens (unless instructed by
the Director); Feeding lines vs memorizing
lines (see more on page 45)

    4. Discuss the movie script, characters,
props, costumes, equipment and locations.
Who is bringing what?

    5. Pass out the production schedule
and copies of the script.

    6. Questions & Answers

    7. Plan next meeting/shoot location.

Chapter Five

Make Your Movie
(Production)

Movie Making Equipment
Video Camera

To shoot a movie, the good news is you do not need all the high tech cameras, lighting, and sound equipment used at Hollywood studios. If you have a consumer camcorder that you are comfortable with, and understand all it offers, then be proud to use it instead of worrying that your camera is not good enough.

Hot Tip!

Make sure to bring your video camera manual to the set EVERYDAY! You never know when a question might arise on how to make your camera operate a certain way and you have no idea which button to push.

Audio

Check to see if you can upgrade the microphone on your camera to improve the audio. Some cameras allow you to attach a "shotgun" microphone. If this is possible, you will want to attach the shotgun microphone to a boom pole that can be extended above the actor's heads to better pick up their lines.

Be sure to check your video camera manual to see if you can manipulate your audio input settings. Some cameras allow you to increase or decrease the volume of the audio. You can also reduce hum's or other low grade frequencies that can interfere with your actor's voices.

Stable Shots and Tripods

Make sure you have a tripod for your camera. Even if you plan a hand held camera shoot, it is a good idea to have a tripod for slower paced scenes where actors won't be moving around the area. Tripods are great for interior scenes where actors are sitting and conversations are the main source of action.

Getting a stable shot can sometimes be very difficult when you are trying to keep your actors motivated, and use available light before it changes. A mono-pod can help with stability (see page 50).

Lighting

Many filmmakers believe lighting a movie set is a science in and of itself. And your camera cannot shoot a scene unless it has light to work with. Even if you do not have special lighting equipment, make sure you understand how to use your camera to increase or decrease its intake of light.

Natural sunlight and interior lights will most likely be enough light for your movie shoot. Never shoot your actors with the light source behind them. This will turn them into giant black shadows, without expressions or personality.

If you want to purchase a "light kit" you will have a greater opportunity to use light to set a mood or an emotional feeling in your scenes. Additional lights indoors can give your scenes a more appealing effect. Lighting used outdoors can soften harsh shadows.

Experiment with lighting to discover how it can make a room creepy or pleasant. How it can turn the ominous shadows under a tree into a softer appearance suitable for a meaningful, emotional scene.

Light kits can be expensive and take many hours to learn how to operate. So consider the costs and your ability to learn how to use this equipment before you bite into your movie budget to buy it.

Other Fun Stuff

Green screens are large sheets of green material that filmmakers drape behind actors which during the editing phase, will be replaced with other video background footage.

In the editing phase, the editor can eliminate the green screen and place any sorts of video images behind the actors. This is an editing technique that is fun and creative and allows you as the director to move your actors to a million and one different locations.

For example, if you want your actors to appear inside a space ship, but you don't have a relative who works for NASA, never fear. Put your actors in front of a green screen, make sure they DO NOT CAST A SHADOW onto the green material, then shoot them saying their lines and acting in the scene.

Have your film editor find footage or a still image of the interior of a space ship (Google "space ship interior" for video or still images).

Using an editing technique, the film editor will remove the green screen from behind the actors and drop in the space ship interior footage. The effect will be that the actors are inside of a space ship!

Movie Making Equipment/Supply List:
Computer with video editing software.
DVD burner, either in your computer
    or external.
Video Camcorder - mini DV is a good
    choice.
Mono pod for your camera.
Mini DV tapes
Headphones
Microphone that attaches to the camera
    for improved audio.
Charged batteries for camcorder.

Other items:
Container for props/costumes.
Make-up kit: Q-tips, kleenex,
    make-up remover
Costumes, props, wigs, hats.

Movie Making Jobs Behind the Camera

If you have friends interested in helping you make your movie, but don't wish to be an actor, here is a list of jobs they can choose from:

Camera Operator - Holds the camera or operates the camera mounted on a tripod. Frames the shot according to the director's instructions. Moves the camera to capture the action and actors. Pushes the record button!

Boom/microphone Operator - Holds the "boom" or the pole with the microphone attached, over the actors heads. Makes certain the microphone is picking up the audio and that it is not getting into the shot. Wears headphones to ensure that the sound is coming through the microphone and into the camera.

Lighting Engineer - If you are using additional lighting equipment, this person must learn the emotional drama of each scene. He or she will visit the scene during the time of day you wish to shoot. They will practice lighting the scene and ensure that the scene is lit and ready when you the director, calls "Action!"

Script Person - Holds the binder that contains the movie script. Keeps track of the progress of the movie shoot, the actors lines (should they forget them), and lets the director know if he or she missed a line or a shot.

Props/Costume Person - Oversees all the costumes and props that are needed for each day of shooting. Makes sure that the props needed for each scene are readily available at the location of the shoot. Makes sure the costumes are in good repair and fit the actors. This person may also visit thrift stores looking for costumes and props.

Make-Up - This is a job that requires an artistic person. He or she will meet with you to discuss the make-up for each actor. The make-up artist must arrive early at each shoot to have enough time to apply the make-up to each actor shooting that day. They will also need to be on hand for any touch ups, as sweat, rain, or other events might ruin an actor's make-up.

Scouting Your Locations
When you are planning your movie,

make sure you have the locations available that are called for in your movie script. But just because you live in a neighborhood surrounded by trees and mountains doesn't mean you can't film a scene that takes place in a desert or on an alien planet.

Is there a play ground nearby with a large sandy area that could become your desert? Or can you shoot the alien planet scene on the tanbark in your friend's back yard? And if you have a green screen (see page 34) you can drop in the desert footage during the editing phase of your movie making.

If you live in a house, apartment, condo or mansion, you have all you need to make a movie. You might need a kitchen for a restaurant scene. Or a bathroom or closet for a scene that takes place inside a prison cell. And if you need a stage for a scene with a singing contest, why not use the hearth in front of a fireplace? Or a deck in the backyard?

The key is to make sure you have permission to shoot wherever you plan to shoot.

Hot Tip!

Keep your locations somewhat close
together, so that if you do forget an
important prop at Scene 2's location yet you
need it for Scene 3's location, it won't take
too long for someone to run and grab it.

Directing Your Actors

How your actors portray their
characters is a result of your ability to direct
them. In other words, it is up to you to
describe (and perhaps even act out) how and
why the character is behaving in each scene.

If a character has just learned their best
friend has been arrested for murder, you
must help your actor find the emotions of
shock, disbelief and fear, so they can
portray those emotions on their face and
with their body and especially in their
voice.

Help your actor by giving them
"motivation." Tell your actor the back
story on why their character behaves and
reacts the way they do. If you explain to
your actor that their character is shocked
and fearful because their accused friend is
diabetic and that being inside a prison cell

could be fatal, your actor will understand better why they must conjure fear, and they will be successful in the scene.

It is also important to bring your listening skills to the scene. Listen to the actors questions. Flesh out their performance with a back and forth discussion. Your actors will appreciate having the chance to "own" their characters. When you yell "action!" and watch as an actor's body, face and voice becomes the characters, you can feel proud that your leadership and communication style has brought about this transformation.

And the movie in your mind is now becoming real right in front of you.

Hot Tip!

Sometimes actors get bored and restless while waiting for the director to get their scenes ready. To keep your actors happy and to avoid them from stomping off the set, have plenty of tasty snacks and cold drinks on hand. Just be sure when you call "Action!" they aren't chewing and their mouths are crumb free!

Directing Your Movie

Your team is assembled and now you must become their captain. Your actors and crew will do their jobs much more effectively if their director has a clear vision of how the movie will look. Know in your mind's eye how the story will be told and how it will unfold.

To be a great director you need to work well with people. It is important that you encourage people with positive comments rather than discouraging them with criticisms. Learn how to compliment them on a job well done. Avoid yelling or name-calling during the movie shoot. Keep your cool and your movie will come to life.

Hot Tip!

Try very hard to keep a smile on my face throughout a movie shoot. A smile goes a long way with actors who are nervous or crew people who are restless.

So, read through your movie script one more time. Review your storyboards one more time. As the director, just like a team captain, you can inspire your team if you thoroughly understand your project and have the clearest vision of how you plan to proceed.

Questions to Ask Yourself:
>Do I know how to light each scene?
Do I know if the costumes are ready for each actor?
Have I picked out the music I want for each scene?
Are the locations picked out and available?
Are the batteries for the video camera fully charged?
Do I have enough video tape?
Do I have enough batteries for the shotgun mic?
Did I confirm with my cast and crew the time and location of our first day of shooting?

The more prepared you are, the better your team will follow your leadership, and the more true your final movie will be. And who benefits the most of all? Your audience!

Movie Director Self Check List:
* You know in your minds eye how your movie will look.

* You are ready to communicate with
    your cast and crew your vision.
* You are confident in the people
    you've chosen for your movie.
* You are prepared to LISTEN.
* You are prepared to inspire others.
* You are prepared to come to
    decisions quickly.

After a day of shooting scenes, it is vitally important that you check all your shot footage (these are called "dailies" or "rushes".) If there are any technical problems such as the audio was dropped or a camera was out of focus, you can make sure to re-shoot these scenes on another day.

Also evaluate the day of shooting: Did it go as planned? Did you run out of time? What were some problems that you can fix for the next day of shooting?

This book will help you make a great movie. If you follow our movie making guidelines, your audiences will love your movie so much, they'll be begging for the sequel.

Important Movie Shooting Hints

As you prepare yourself to shoot a movie, make sure your camera is loaded with film, and the lens is clean. Is the scene set? Are the props you'll need available and at hand? Are the actors in costume and make-up? Call the first actors to the set. Issue the all important command of "Quiet on the set!"

Now make sure the shot is framed correctly. Imagine a picture frame encircling your actors as they are positioned on the set. Refer to your storyboard to help remind you how you originally envisioned the scene. If all is perfect, call "Action!"

Hot Tip!

The director calling "Action!" is not only important to give the actors their cue that it's time to act, the word "Action!" is also useful when you are in the edit room in post production. As you roll through the footage, you know you don't need what is right before the word "Action!" In fact, you know to cut the footage right after the word can be heard. This will help your editing process go smoothly and quickly.

If your actors have memorized their lines, the scenes will flow much better as the actors talk to each other, back and forth. But if your actors have not memorized their lines, do not panic.

You as the director can feed them their lines, one by one. Here is how you will do this:

Feeding Lines:
Have your script person stand next to you holding the script open to the correct page. You will read out loud the line you want your actor to say. You might say the line with the emotions you wish the actor to portray.

Always at the end of giving them their line, say "Action." The reason you need to say "action" is especially important during editing. When you are editing the movie, your own voice saying "action" will help you know when to cut footage. Also, the actor will pause before they deliver their line, waiting for you to say "action." This allows you to readjust your shoot angle.

This is because, when feeding lines,

after each line you must change the camera angle. An actor cannot stay perfectly still. They will move and change position during the course of several lines. If you shoot the actor at the same angle during a series of lines, on screen the actor bounces in an incomprehensible fashion. So, when the actor is about to say their second line, change your angle. When you are in a good position, and the actor has been "fed" their next line, say "action."

The trick is to stay close enough to the speaking actor, so the microphone can pick up their voice. Angles should be realistic, nothing too wild such as shooting from above or below them.

Depending on how strong your actors are, as you "feed" them their lines, you may find yourself acting the line with the emotions and movements necessary to properly portray the character.

After the line is said by the actor, do a quick evaluation before moving on to the next line:
Did the actor say the line properly?
Was their voice strong enough?

Was the actor NOT looking at the
camera?
Was the emotion appropriate (no
smiling!)
Were you shooting from a fresh angle?
Was the camera on "REC" for record?

If you feel the need to redo the line,
this is when you do it. Once your actors get
the hang of it, movie making goes very
quickly.

Hot Tip!

Think about consistency: Does your movie
take place over one day, a week or a year?
If it is during one day, make sure your
actor's make-up, costumes (and hair - no
haircuts until AFTER the movie is 'in the
can') remain CONSISTENT, especially if
you are shooting their scenes on different
days. They must wear the same clothes for
each scene, unless the script calls for them
to change.

Camera Moves:
Decide if you want your scene shot
STATIONARY, on a tripod not moving;
HAND-HELD, your camera operator is
holding the camera and moving as you

direct him or her; or MOVING, usually the camera operator is riding on a wheeled cart, skateboard, or even from inside a car.

Camera Angles:
Close-up of the speaking actor (approx. 2 feet away).
Long shot of the speaking actor (approx. 4 feet away).
Behind the speaking actor's head, capturing the actor who is being spoken to.
You can use these same angles over and over again, just make sure to mix them up.

Types of Shots:
Usually at the opening of a scene, your audience needs to understand where the action is happening. This first shot you should shoot is called the "establishing shot."

To help them know where the story is taking place, you can make signs such as "Beauty Shop" or "Meditation Center" or "Coffee Cafe." Then shoot a long shot (establishing shot), capturing the entire location and actors involved, then zoom in on the signs.

LONG SHOT - Includes all the actors and background of a scene.

MEDIUM SHOT - Upper body of an actor.

CLOSE-UP - A small part of the actor such as face, hands, feet.

EXTREME CLOSE-UP - Very close to an actor, such as zooming in on a sweaty upper lip.

The camera can reveal things only the audience sees, and the actors appear unaware. Shoot from behind a "bad guy" who is spying at a group of characters, who are completely unaware that danger is nearby.

Other typical camera moves:

PAN - Following someone who is walking or running across the scene.

TILT - An up and down movement such as when a character is jumping on or off an object. This move is mostly done while a camera is on a tripod.

ZOOM - Unfortunately most people use the zoom too often. Use the zoom sparingly, and your audience will thank you.

Steady Shots:

Other than using a tripod, getting a steady shot without expensive equipment is very difficult.

A mono pod is an inexpensive way to steady your shots. With the camera mounted on the mono pod, you can carry it quickly from shot to shot, extending the leg to the ground for stabilizing. Also, when you retract the leg, holding the mono pod as a base, it acts as a stabilizer.

Framing the Shot:

Think of this as the composition of a picture. If the objects in your frame are centered and balanced, they will also be boring. But if you frame your shot a little off center, the shot becomes more interesting. It also helps your audience to understand the mood you want to set. A little unbalance helps a comedy scene appear more funny!

Bloopers!

Kids and audiences LOVE bloopers! They seem to look forward to the bloopers showing at the end of the movie, almost more than the movie itself! At the cast meeting, tell the cast to expect plenty of natural bloopers. To not waste time, urge your cast to not fake any goof-ups. The bloopers can be edited into the movie at the end, during or after the credits roll.

During shooting when a blooper does occur (mustaches falling off, stuffed animals falling out of windows, and dozens of flubbed up lines), it is great to let the cast have a good laugh. Let the camera roll during the enjoyment of the blooper. Include the laughter and enjoyment when editing the blooper. Your audience will laugh even harder!

Special Effects While Shooting:
If you need to have an actor appear or disappear, simply secure the position of the camera and the shot, with the appropriate background. Shoot for 10 seconds. To have a character suddenly appear, have the actor walk into the shot. Direct them to stand exactly where you wish them to appear. Hold the shot for 10 seconds.

To have someone disappear, reverse these steps. Position the camera to shoot the actor for ten seconds. Ask the actor to leave the shot. Shoot the empty space for 10 more seconds.

The special effects are added during editing.

Chase Scenes:
Set up the camera pointing towards the background you wish to shoot. Have the characters run towards and past the camera. The camera does not move.

Sound Effects:
Often sounds need to be re-created then later added to your movie during the editing phase.

How can you record thunder and lightening for your scene when outside it is a beautiful October day? Ask yourself what else makes the sounds of thunder and lightening? (hint: a sheet of metal and a wooden spoon!)

If you need the sound of footsteps on a rainy, gravel walkway, have a friend put on a pair of boots, hose down a gravel walkway and hold the camera near his feet recording him as he deliberately takes each crunching step.

For the sounds of a sword battle, have your parents supervise while you use a knife and a knife sharpener clashing them together near the camera's microphone.

Again, let your imagination take over on how ordinary objects can be used to re-create the sounds your movie needs to tell the story effectively.

Chapter Six

Edit Your Movie
(Post-Production)

For movie editing software, we recommend iMovie from Apple. This program is simple to learn and easy to use. Go to www.apple.com to find out how to purchase iMovie or what type of computer you will need to use iMovie AND to burn DVD's.

Another editing program that we recommend from Apple is Final Cut Express or Final Cut Pro. For users of iMovie, it is very easy to advance to these more sophisticated and stable platforms.

Apple's DVD creation and burning software is iDVD or DVD Studio Pro. Again, these are easy to use and offer a variety of menus and templates to choose from.

This book does not coach you through the editing process. Your software will come with a handbook which we recommend you use to learn the functions of your video editing software.

But still, here are a few tips that will help you as you go through the editing process:

1. Editing takes many hours. Accept this and you won't get burned out.

2. Make sure you have enough space on your computer hard drive before you import your video footage.

3. Import your footage by connecting your computer to your camera with a firewire cable. Turn the camcorder on and launch your video editing software. Name each clip before you import them.

4. Place your clips into the timeline which is the sequence of events you wish your movie to appear. You can also trim your clips while they are in the timeline, removing unwanted pieces of video and audio.

5. Once your movie clips are in order on the timeline, you can add transitions and

special effects.

6. Lay down the music you've chosen.
Hopefully it is original music and not music
you would need to license to receive
approval to use. *(See the back of this book for
information about music).*

7. Add the sound effects you created.

8. Add narration or voice overs.

9. Type in the credits. Make sure all your
cast and crew names are spelled correctly.

Chapter Seven

Premier Your Movie

Your movie is "in the can." You successfully edited the footage and now it is burned onto a DVD. The next step is to show it to the world.

You can certainly upload it to YouTube, and announce its availability to every living person you know. Plus you can host a premier, showing the movie to a live audience.

If you are a community activist, you might consider showing your movie as a fundraiser. You can choose a charity, sell tickets and donate the money back to the charity.

You can enter your movie into film festivals. Check out the website Withoutabox for information on national and international film festivals: https://www.withoutabox.com/

You can offer to show your movie as an activity during lunch or after school.

Make enough DVD's for each of your cast and crew members. They too can spread the word about the movie, providing the YouTube URL to all their friends on Facebook and e-mail.

As word spreads, who knows - maybe a Hollywood producer or distributor will take an interest in your movie or your talents and give you your lucky break!

Shelley's Green light

I have nurtured my Make-A-Movie business for the past five years, showing children as young as five years old, that they too can act and star in a movie with a great story line, titles, credits, special effects and bloopers! Now you have in your hands the how-to's to become a movie director and make movies starring your friends and family - and pets!

I hope that you will relish your role as a movie director. After all, you are providing your friends and family members with an incredibly fun and unique activity.

Plus you will learn many things about yourself in the process of making your own movie - your creativity, leaderships skills, self motivation and patience. And once you have your movie in the form of a DVD resting in your hot little hand, your sense of accomplishment will be something you can be proud of.

You've got the green light, so go out and make some movies!

-Shelley Frost
shelley@makeamoviestudios.com

Sample Movie Making Materials
Appendix I.

Sample pages from Make-A-Movie Studios movie scripts:

"A Spy in Mozambula"
15 minute movie after editing

"The Stroke of Midnight"
30 minute movie after editing

"A Spy in Mozambula"
<u>10 - 12 cast members</u>
Script Description:
Agent Major and Agent Minor are determined to protect the President of Mozambula from BBG (Big Bad Guy) and his henchman who are out to steal the diamonds the President will display at his upcoming speech. But when Queen Latofu and a radical environmental activist show up, the Mozambula animals are scared stiff!

Scene 1: A Corridor. Agent Major is battling several Henchmen.

Agent Major
It's taken ten years, but I always knew I'd smoke out your boss, Big Bad Guy also known as BBG!

Henchman #1
Yeah? Well you ain't gettin' anywhere's near our boss!

Action: Agent Major does karate moves on Henchman #1

Henchman #2
BBG is way outta your league, Agent!
Action: Agent Major does karate moves Henchman #2

Henchman #1
That's right, Agent. BBG's criminal mind is too brilliant!

Action: Agent Major does karate moves on Henchman #3

<u>Henchman #2</u>
Yeah, and he's smart too!

Action: Agent Major does karate
moves on Henchman #4

<u>Henchman #1</u>
Yeah, you'd never understand 'em -
right guys? Let's get him!

Action: All four corner Agent Major.
Just when they're about to tackle
Agent Major, his cell phone rings.
They stop in surprise and look at
each other. Agent Major answers his
phone.

<u>Agent Major</u>
Hey Agent Minor, how're you doing?

Action: Using the element of surprise,
Agent Major karate chops two
Henchmen. They're out cold.

<u>Agent Minor (on the phone in another
area)</u>

Hey Boss, did I catch you at a bad time?

Agent Major
Naw - it's been pretty slow.

Action: Agent Major does karate moves on the two remaining Henchmen. They're out cold.

Agent Major
But thanks for checking in, Agent Minor. You're a great partner - always there when I need you.

Action: Agent Major uses his cell phone to clunk a moving Henchman on the head. He's out cold.

Action: Agent Major's phone rings again. It's the Chief back at Headquarters.

Agent Major
Agent Major here.

Chief's Voice
Agent Major! Get yourself to
Mozambula, Africa. Looks like BBG is
headed there to cook up more
trouble.

Agent Major
I'm on my way Chief.

Action: Looking into the camera with
a smile.

An African Safari... the only trophy I
want... is BBG!

"The Stroke of of Midnight"
11 Cast members
Script Description:
Gathered around a campfire, ghost
stories are being told to a group of
campers. When it's Richard's turn, he
tells them his story is true. It all
began 500 years ago when three
warlocks captured the Boogyman
and his Boogeyboys in a raging
battle. They imprisoned them in a

back room of their cottage - a cottage coveted by three homeless witches. Will the witches succeed in evicting the warlocks from their home? Will the Boogeyman escape in time to scare the children at Halloween? And how does Richard fit into this horror story? The end will send you screaming from the room!

SCENE 1. Campfire: A group of kids are sitting around a campfire roasting marshmallows. Around them, the dark forest vibrates with howling creatures and rustling tees. The mood of the campers has gone from merry to scary as they listen intently to one young man telling a horrifying tale.

<u>Kayla</u>
Gee, it's kinda spooky out here tonight.

<u>Chris</u>
Nothing to worry about. Last I

heard, Big foot was a fake (laughs)

Kelly
Kayla, I'm with you. This place is giving me the creeps.

Nick
Hey Richard. Let's tell some ghost stories and really scare the girls!

Jeeyna
Too late, I already got scared looking at you (sticking her tongue out at Nick)

Richard
Well campers, since this is our last night at Camp Winihaka, I think we should have a storytelling hour. But nothing too scary (little laugh). Why don't I tell the first story... a true story... well as a matter of fact... it's about something that happened to me...

Action: The kids lean in as if

captivated by what Richard is telling them.

FLASHBACK BEGINS: Lawyers
Office. Richard is seated while the lawyer is reading from a will.

<u>Lawyer</u>
So you see Richard, your great uncle, Richard Boogman, has bequested to you the Boogman family home.

<u>Richard</u>
I didn't even know there was a Boogman family home. And since when did I even have a Great Uncle.

<u>Lawyer (clearing his throat)</u>
Well, actually, now that he is deceased, you no longer have an uncle. I'm sorry about that. But you are now the owner of 666 Haunted Lane.

<u>Richard</u>
Haunted Lane? Isn't that a little

foreboding?

<u>Lawyer</u>
Oops - did I say Haunted? Ha, ha, I
meant Hunter Lane. Uh, here's the
deed and the key to the house. Oh,
and you may have this plant as a
housewarming gift from me.
Richard takes the plant, the key and
the deed a bit awkwardly.

<u>Richard (As he leaves the office)</u>
Gee, thanks.

Appendix II.

Music Resources:

Garageband
http://www.apple.com/ilife/garageband/

Jamendo
http://www.jamendo.com/en/

Freeplay
http://freeplaymusic.com/

Music Bakery
http://musicbakery.com/

Helpful Movie Making Resources:

The Artists Rights Foundation
        MAKING MOVIES: A Guide for
Young Filmmakers,
http://www.asiaing.com/making-movies-a-
guide-for-young-filmmakers.html

Movie Maker: The Art and Business of
Making Movies,
www.moviemaker.com

Make-A-Movie Studios,
www.makeamoviestudios.com

Appendix III.

Sample Production Schedule of the Make-
A-Movie movie script
"The Fowl Phobia"

Summer Movie 2008
Shoot Schedule

Monday, July 7th
Scene 1: The Library
Characters
Gilbert
Whistler

Props
Duster
Shusher

Scene 2: Coat room/Research Librarian Desk
Characters
Gilbert
Jane Smith

Props
Disguise

Flashback Scene:

Characters
Gilbert
Helen Halifax

Props
cell phones
books

Tuesday, July 8th

Scene 4: Library/front door/
research desk
Characters
Gilbert disguised
Jane
Whistler
Julius Caesar
Cleopatra
Sleeping Beauty
Mona Lisa
Tinker bell with wand
Helen Halifax

Props
Shusher
books
World Atlas
newspapers
magazines
overturned books
Sign Town Library

Mona Lisa Poster

Wednesday, July 9th

Scene 3: Library

<u>Characters</u>
Gilbert
Jane Smith

<u>Props</u>
Signs
Mona Lisa Poster

Scene 5: Outside Library Front Lawn

<u>Characters</u>
Gilbert
Mrs. Halifax
Whistler

<u>Props</u>
Library Sign

Scene 6: Library

<u>Characters</u>
Gilbert
Whistler
Eleanor
Caesar
Cleopatra
Sleeping Beauty
Mona Lisa
Tinker bell

Props
grapes
make-up
handbag
fairy dust
brooms, mops, dusters
Clutter of magazines, etc

Thursday, July 10th
Scene 7: Library Interior
Characters
ALL

Props
Two Starbucks coffee containers
Shusher
Big Blue Ribbon

Cast Credits!!

Appendix IIII.

Storyboard Squares. Copy these onto
several sheets of paper, and begin
diagraming your movie scenes.

ABOUT THE AUTHOR

Shelley Frost is the co-author of two books, *Throw Like a Girl: Discovering the Body, Mind & Spirit of the Athlete in You* (Beyond Words, 2000) and *Your Adopted Dog: Everything You Need to Know About Rescuing & Adopting a Best Friend in Need* (The Lyons Press, 2007).

She also teaches acting and drama through the San Carlos Children's Theater and in her own Make-A-Movie Workshops.

Shelley is also a professional videographer, producing documentaries and promotional videos for non-profit organizations.

Shelley has appeared on Oprah, Dateline NBC and in People Magazine as well as numerous television and radio programs.